YEŞİL EV

A HOME

To Mrs Moreen Hughes

with the best wishes
of the author.

21/7/2.-

PUBLISHED BY:
TÜRKİYE TURİNG VE OTOMOBİL KURUMU
JANUARY 1999

TRANSLATED BY: ADAIR MILL

ISBN 975 - 7641 - 29 - 4

PRINTED BY
ANA BASIM A.Ş.
0 (212) 276 23 14

TTOK
1. Oto Sanayi Sitesi Yanı, Çamlık Caddesi No: 2
4. Levent - İSTANBUL / TURKEY
Ph: 0 (212) 282 81 40 (7 Lines)
Telefax: 0 (212) 282 80 42

YEŞİL EV
Sultanahmet - İSTANBUL / TURKEY
Ph: 0 (212) 517 67 85 (4 Lines)
Telefax: 0 (212) 517 67 80

This book has been dedicated to all friends of "Yeşil Ev" in the world.
Friends; all human being whom loved and enjoyed the humanity of this house, it's interior historical and art beauties, it's ease and peacefull atmosphere and the tastes of trees and flowers in it's garden.

Çelik Gülersoy

YEŞİL EV

A HOME

İSTANBUL
1999

Throughout the whole of history, capital cities have possessed one distinguishing feature in common: Wherever the royal dynasty resides, in whatever district the "royal court" may be located, the same vicinity will also be chosen by the high dignitaries of state for their seats of residence, with the result that it is in this particular district that the finest architecture and the most magnificent buildings are to be found.

This same feature was to be observed in the Istanbul of the Roman and Byzantine periods. The palaces occupied over the centuries by the Emperors formed a complex extending from the south of the Hippodrome to the shores of the Marmara, and it was in this quarter and the surrounding district that the mansions of the high dignitaries of state and wealthy citizens were located. They were also concentrated on the left, seaward side of the Mese street a little further off.

Immediately after the Conquest, the young Mehmet II built a wooden palace at Beyazıt, but later transferred his residence to the hill on which the acropolis of pagan Byzantion had stood. It now seems quite incomprehensible that the later Christian Roman and Byzantine Emperors should have rejected the Acropolis as a site for their palaces in favor of slopes overlooking the dull and monotonous landscape of the Marmara, for the ancient Acropolis occupied a quite extraordinary location, with the Golden Horn on its left, the Bosphorus in front and the Sea of Marmara on the right.

The real reason that attracted the emperors to the other side was probably of a socio-political nature: to be near the Hippodrome which constituted the main meeting-place and the main centre of entertainment of the people, and so keep it under their control.

The Ottoman Sultans preferred the locality now known as Seraglio Point, with the result that, during the period that lasted until the middle of the 19th century, the district just beyond, on the slopes overlooking the Marmara between Sultanahmet and Beyazıt, gradually became covered with the mansions of the various statesmen and court dignitaries.

At the beginning of the 19th century the situation was transformed by the transfer of the imperial household to the shores of the Bosphorus. The old wooden palace at Dolmabahçe was demolished during the 1840s and replaced in 1856 by the new Dolmabahçe Palace, the first of a line of new, magnificent European type stone-built buildings, to be followed by the Çerağan Palace between Beşiktaş and Ortaköy, the Beylerbeyi Palace and the Küçüksu Kasrı on the other side of the Bosphorus and, later, by the Palace at Yıldız. The construction of these new palaces, combined with the final abandonment of Topkapı Sarayı as the royal residence, encouraged the court officials and high dignitaries to choose sites for their residences in these new areas, at Maçka, Nişantaşı and Teşvikiye for the Dolmabahçe Palace, and, for the later palace at Yıldiz, the slopes of Yıldız and Serencebey.

That the Sublime Porte, the office of the Grand Vizier, remained in its ancient place in Sirkeci prevented the complete abandonment of the then select residential area of Kadırga and Beyazıt, and, although the viziers themselves may have left, the lower ranks of high government officials still remained in the old districts.

The mansion that forms the topic of this booklet, the house belonging to the Regie Nazırı (Director of Monopoly) Şükrü Bey, could, if we may use a contemporary idiom, be classified as being in the "second division". In other words, although not on the same scale as the magnificent konaks of the highest dignitaries, it was much superior to the dwellings of the common people.

Although Şükrü Bey could boast the title "Nazır", normally the equivalent of the English "Minister", his particular post was more in the nature of the director of a government body, rather like the general manager of a state enterprise at the present day.

In the Şükrü Bey Konağı, the main entrance was opening into a marble paved hall from which doors gave access to the harem and selâmlık sections. I imagine that the women must have occupied the side looking out on to Sultanahmet Mosque while the men occupied the side facing Ayasofya. The ground floor consisted of this marble entrance hall, the staircases on each side, and a sofa opposite opening on to the garden. The first floor contained low-ceilinged rooms providing accommodation for the servants, while the high-ceilinged salon on the upper floor looked out, not on to the garden, but on to the narrow street and the Ayasofya Hamamı.

At the beginning of the 20th century, this wooden konak, built towards to the end of the 19th, was confronted with a development that was to have unfortunate consequences not only for the mansion itself but also for the whole of the surrounding district:

It was decided to build a prison right opposite Ayasofya.

In the previous fifty or sixty years the area had declined to such an extent that when it became necessary to build a prison somewhere in Istanbul this probably suggested itself as the most obvious choice of location.

The main factor in the choice of the area was, however, that the site between that particular corner and Topkapı Palace, which had been considered in the 1840s as a possible site for the University and which was later used for the National Assembly, was at that time occupied by the lawcourts.

In Şükrü Bey's konak, with its latticed windows and, introverted air, the necessary precautions were immediately taken against their vulgar, disagreeable neighbour. A wall was built across the spacious garden at the back, thus protecting the house from the inauspicious sight of the nearby prison-house.

From this event, in 1910's, until the 1970s, life went on as usual in the konak. Old people died and young people grew old. With the death of the General Director the konak lost its main source of revenue and the great house gradually fell into a state of neglect and dilapidation.

While a student at the Faculty of Law in the 1950s I used to enjoy walking here from Beyazıt, and I would often stand gazing at this great wooden house in this narrow, deserted street.

The tomb on its eastern side still preserved its old other-worldly air, while the medrese on the west, on the side looking towards Sultanahmet Mosque, was visibly crumbling into ruin, deteriorating with every passing year.

The medrese was to fall victim to a fate worse than mere ruin. It was to be the victim of a perfectly legal piece of foul play. Although, as a Vakıf, or pious foundation, the building ought to have been preserved as a whole for all time, somehow or other, at some date or other, the front part of the noble stone building was sold off to private individuals and converted into a line of horrible concrete shops, losing all its distinctive architectural character.

As a final insult, at the end of this side of the konak garden the family built later a carpenter's workshop and rented it out.

My heart bled to see the building declining further into ruin each year, but in 1958 my studies ended and in the 1960s increasing pressure of work made me a stranger to the district.

In 1971, I was responsible for a very important development in the Institution in which I held an executive post. A reform in the institution (and in the country at large) assured it a very substantial revenue: Turks resident abroad had to take out a temporary import for their vehicles when visiting this country.

In return for its role as guarantor to the state, the Association gained a very considerable (and completely unexpected) source of income. The news of our new-found wealth spread abroad, and various people began to offer their property for sale to the Association.

From 1973-1976 I was obliged to spend a great deal in waging a sort of civil war within the association itself, against to the privat aims, and during this "interregnum" we lost the opportunity of buying a number of valuable properties at a very low price.

In 1977, by a stroke of good fortune, this konak was offered for sale! The offer was made by the family lawyer Taner Saka to our own lawyer, my good friend Nezihî Sanal.

And it was because of this that, one morning, I went back to see my old love, this old wooden konak.

The front part of the house, the side towards the street, still preserved something of its original character, though much deteriorated.

But the interior, and the rear and side facades were in a really horrendous state, while on the garden side, the once magnificent mansion was no better than a great ruined poultry coop. The garden was a barren waste. You can see this from the photographs.

The price proposed was "reasonable" for the time and we decided to purchase it.

The price was reasonable for the time, i.e. for the 1970s, when speculation had not yet driven property values sky-high and raised prices far beyond world standards, and when finance-capital still remained within legal limits and "dirty money" had not yet become an accepted feature of our economic life. (The value in dollars was 350.000.).

The money was very available, but the decision required courage.

For one thing, the area in which the property was located was no better than a refuse dump, and the last place to come to mind when thinking of tourism. And the fact that it was a "listed building" was really the last straw, making it impossible to embark on new construction or to enlarge the building in any way. In other words, it could had twenty rooms and twenty rooms it had to stay.

For a touristic establishment, a building of this size could serve merely as a services wing or an annex.

Thus our decision to invest in this property was looked upon as sheer madness in financial circles or, to put it more kindly, as another of the Touring Association's "Director's caprices or utopian dreams". My decision two years later to take over ruined pavilions slumbering in dark and deserted woods and groves on distant hills in other parts of the city was to meet with the same reaction, but later, when they had fully repaid the investment on the cultural side and also, to a certain extent, on the economic, they were to become objects of general admiration.

But things that appear quite irrational when viewed from the purely financial and feasibility-profitability point of view, appear quite differently when viewed from the point of view of culture and touristic enterprise, and one realises that in some things one must take a bold step "in spite of everything".

Such self-sacrifice should fall either to the state or to a non-profit making charitable institution. If we had been living in the Turkey of the 1920s or the 1930s, the task would have been undertaken by the idealistic state of those days.

At that time, tourism had not yet made its appearance on the national agenda, but the concept of the state as regards its obligation to the nation made decisions such as this quite an everyday event. But by the 1970s the political environment in Turkey had been completely transformed and the state no longer played a leading role in such matters.

But as a non-profit organization, we had a little money in hand (as far as the market was concerned never too much) and I felt convinced that it was up to our Association to undertake this task.

Since the trying days of the 1970's the main organs of the Association, the Executive Committee and the General Assembly, had been composed of educated and cultured individuals with no eye to personal profit, and they now unhesitantly supported my idea of investing in an area that in appearance was the most derelict part of Istanbul but which its historical identity made potentially the richest and the most dynamic.

(This decision was later shown to be justified from the economic point of view too. The revenue from the hotel in those fourteen years is practically nothing compared to the capital actually invested. In the last few years, and particularly since the near-by prison was taken over by an international hotel company, speculative investment has turned to this area, and here, as on the Bosphorus and in other modern areas, property prices have simply rocketed. If, at any time, the Association should be obliged to part with this property too, the profit would more than make up for the low revenue of the intervening years.)

But let us come back to our story.

We paid the money and purchased the site with cultural and touristic advantages in mind rather than financial profit.

But for five years we were unable to embark on the necessary construction work.

At that time, our construction programme was headed by the rebuilding of the customs entry post at the Bulgarian border, a project I regarded, from the material point of view, as an essential requirement for the workers entering Turkey from abroad, and, at the same time, as a moral obligation on our part to those who were providing us with our main source of revenue. This "window opening on to the West" was a dust bowl in summer and a sea of mud in winter. A certain amount of work had been done on it, but it still remained a mere building site. It consisted of only three lanes, and was, in any case, based on a wholly mistaken principle: Traffic entering from the right was shunted over to the left, the formalities were planned in a future central building, the travellers making their way there carrying their luggage in their hands, and then, when everything was finished, the stream of traffic was directed back to the right. The first large investment using our new, and large revenue had, for several years, to be concentrated here, in the Kapıkule project, and our other projects, including the revitalisation of the derelict building in Sultanahmet, simply had to wait.

After the military coup in 1980 it looked as if technical projects like Kapıkule as well as cultural-touristic projects such as Sultanahmet would all have to be abandoned. The Ministry of Tourism set its mind on channeling to itself the source of revenue which the Association had recently acquired. They persuaded the generals to accept the idea and a law was passed to that effect.

This decision not only shattered my dreams, it effectively put an end to the Association.

But there was one obstacle that stood in the way of the realisation of their plan. Our Association had acquired international status as a legal body, and, since 1930, had been linked as guarantor with other international tourism-automobile associations. It was thus impossible, by means of a unilateral decision on the part of the Turkish government to remove our Association from the chain and insert a state institution in its place. This would have caused very great problems for transit traffic through Turkey and for international commercial traffic leaving Turkey for countries abroad. The situation was explained by me to the highest échelon of government and, after what were, for me, months of worry and anxiety, the decision, which had been passed into law but not put into effect, was repealed by a new law restoring our 1930 status.

But in doing us this favor, the highest "échelons" of the state expected the Association to continue in the direction begun in 1979, namely, giving priority to investments in state property and to the repair and revitalisation of ruined or derelict parks and pavilions, at the Bosphorus.

As these "state demands" fitted in exactly with our own inclinations we were only too pleased to give priority to these in 1981 and 1982, postponing for two years any investment in the Association's own properties.

In 1983 I at last put Sultanahmet on the agenda. Funds were allocated and, at last, work could begin on the construction. But how exactly was this to be carried out?

In those days there was no definite architectural categorization of old buildings. An old building was either repaired, which was very exception, or left to fall gradually into ruin, after which it would be replaced by a concrete apartment block with no relation to the former building. We ourselves have been responsible for the formulation of the "Class II listed building" concept. I explained to the High Commission for Ancient Monuments that if we were given permission to demolish the building and construct a new building identical with the old on the outside, then we would have the opportunity of revitalising the last old building in the district. Otherwise, it would collapse and a concrete apartment block would be constructed in its place. Professor Doğan Kuban, the Chairman of the Executive Committee of the Commission, was a member of our Association and a personal friend. He was also a scholar and a lover of art. He came and saw things for himself, and the Commission accepted the Association's proposal.

The plan was produced by our architect, Mustafa Pehlivanoğlu and was his first undertaking. He remained so faithful to the old building that even although it would have been very advantageous for the hotel if the ceiling on the first floor had been raised a few inches he refused to make the change and kept strictly to the old measurements. The exterior was, in any case, an exact replica of the old. The only material change in the interior was the removal of one of the two staircases at two sides of the building. The upper floor salon was transformed into a "suite". This was christened the "Pasha Bedroom", since the term "royal suite" usually used in hotels was scarcely suitable here.

The building was finally completed in 1984 and presented to the world like a lovely cake!

And now let us make a "sociological" digression of this "lovely cake"

From the point of view of cultural

concepts such as urban history and identity, it would have been greatly preferable to have left the old wooden building as it was and to have confined the work to a through restoration. A wooden building that was meant as a dwelling for a very small number of people could never serve as a hotel used for the accommodation of a large number of guests, but, simply restored, it could have been given a suitable function, such as a museum. That is what would have been done in most European cities.

But East is East and West is West, and there are many great differences between the two, the most important being the construction material employed in domestic architecture. The "settled" nature of European life has resulted in the choice of stone as the main building material.

In the East, and in Istanbul in particular, wood has been preferred, partly because of the nomadic roots of the people, partly because of the comparative cheapness of the material. But wood is particularly liable to damage from snow and rain and the passage of time.

Moreover, the concept of maintenance, the idea of prolonging the life of a building by giving it the necessary care and repair, is a predominantly Western characteristic, again stemming from the adoption of a settled life-style. To the oriental, the idea of "maintenance" is totally foreign.

To these social factors may be added an economic one. The decline in the Ottoman economy over the last two centuries of the Empire affected every aspect of society, and the imperial capital, together with the financial status of the family, fell into terminal decline.

Still another factor is the cultural change that has taken place in the last 100-150 years. In accordance with new value judgments and new standards of taste, old buildings were looked upon as old-fashioned and everyone turned to newer, more modern constructions.

In spite of the accumulation of all these factors, the Şükrü Bey Konağı was able to struggle on bravely for sixty or seventy years and then, in the 1970s, fell into complete ruin.

The building we took over in 1977 was far beyond repair or restoration .

The demolition of a wooden building and its replacement by a new concrete building faced with wood to make it resemble the old, is far from ideal. That is only too obvious.

But we, the administrators of the 1970s, could offer a perfectly good excuse.

A building identical with the old is to be regarded as at least a sort of consolation and as performing a service to the city landscape.

As I stressed in our booklet on The Street of "Soğukçeşme", the creation of old models using modern techniques and new materials allows the urban identity to survive at least in outward appearance. In other words, the city landscape is saved.

As wood is no longer viable as a building material, we must at least do our best to save appearances.

Before the conversion of the old building had been fully completed but when the new structure had already begun to take shape it was time to turn our attention to the garden, and that is when I personally took over. I let the great fig tree stay but had the other gnarled old trees cut down, replacing them with healthy limes, planes and horse chestnuts . I built a conservatory-salon towards the east, and set a monumental cascade in the west corner. In the middle of the wall I placed an absolutely unique object - a cistern for storing water or snow covered with reliefs symbolising rain and water. Behind the great Serasker Konağı at Yıldız, demolished in the 1920s, there was a smaller subsidiary konak in which I myself grew up and which Reşit Saffet Atabinen, the founder chairman of our Association, entered as son-in-law in 1917. It was in the garden of this last konak that this Byzantine relic used to lie. It had been found buried in the garden of the house at Dolmabahçe, at the top of the slope on the Ayazpaşa side, which had belonged to Atabinen's grandfather. Many years later, Reşit Bey had the antique piece transferred to Yıldız. On Atabinen's death in 1965, the son-in-law of the family sold it to the antique dealers Sevsevil Brothers in Zincirli Han in the Grand Bazaar. I went and found it there, purchased it at a very reasonable price and had it brought to the garden at Sultanahmet.

This gave me a very bright idea. The middle of the garden behind the Yeşil Ev was empty and called for an architectural decor rather than an ordinary tree. The very thing, and something truly monumental, was lying at Yıldız.

This was the pink porphyry pool, of

Italian workmanship, that had stood in the rear garden of a block of flats erected on one of the lots into which the land once occupied by the Serasker Konağı, with its eighty or ninety rooms, had been divided after the demolition of the great mansion.

I went there with Bukan Ersu, a friend of the children of the family and chief accountant in the Association, and put in a bid for the piece. The family were very happy to be rid of this "impediment" right in the centre of the little garden that cut down the "playing space", and the price they asked was very reasonable: TL 500,000.- the equivalent of $. 26.000 at that time.

We spent that much again on dismantling and re-erecting it. But it was still a very good bargain.

The transport of the marble by lorry was quite an adventure. An over-officious citizen phoned the police to say that "an antique sculpture was being smuggled abroad". The Beşiktaş police immediately took action (if only they were as quick to act on other occasions!), stopped the lorry and detained the architect and the workers.

This happened in 1983. By that time my name had already become well known in connection with the restoration of Yıldız Park and the pavilions there. When the police superindent heard my name, he declared that "that man wouldn't do such a thing" and gave the architect permission to telephone to us (a remarkable exception for a police station). And that was how I learned of the incident. It was a Saturday and the office was closed.. I had it opened up, and since there was, of course, no secretary, I typed a petition with one finger, signed it and sent to the police. And so we rescued the pool, our architect and the workers.

I have related these stranger than fiction events as amusing anecdotes. But they also serve to show the serious difficulties one has to be prepared to face in such enterprises.

I furnished the interior "in the style of the period", the first time such a thing had been attempted in Turkey. I rummaged through antique shops to find brass bedsteads and collected engravings and coloured lithographs, which, at that time, could still be found at quite reasonable prices.

I chose a different colour for each room (blue, green, beige, etc,) and furnished them with tasselled velvet curtains and carpets to match.

The "Pasha Bedroom", with its much larger dimensions, demanded a much more impressive decor. Here again, the Serasker Konağı came to the rescue. The stone konak that had survived from that palatial building was the house that Reşit Saffet Bey, the founder of our Association and the man who had been responsible for my upbringing in my childhood years, entered as a son-in-law in 1917. His father-in-law, Şükrü Pasha, the Serasker's second son, was posted as military attaché to Vienna and, on his return to the capital, brought back a lacquer and gilt bedroom suite for his daughter Nurhayat Hanımefendi's trousseau. When this konak too, the last of the great old mansions, was demolished in 1969 the family were at a loss as to where to store this magnificent bedroom suite. I asked if I could have it. Gültekin Taneri, their daughter and a very close childhood friend of my own, with typical nobility and generosity quoted a purely nominal price. I bought the suite and had it placed in the Pasha Bedroom, producing a decor absolutely without parallel in Istanbul.

The colour I chose for the building, a special shade of green, caused quite a furore in "super-intellectual" circles. Even a female writer of novels of the "the moon went behind a cloud and he kissed her" variety was quite shocked. These were all children of Istanbul's derelict period, and to them an old building was a broken down ruin with its wood blackened with rain and snow or a building painted in red ochre. They had no idea of the yellow, pink, straw and tender green colours that from the Tulip Period onwards had transformed the capital of the Empire into a bed of flowers.

Nevzat Ayaz, the then Governor of Istanbul, unwilling to offend me, asked me very tactfully the reason for my choice of colour. In reply, I reminded him with a light melancholie of an old Istanbul song:

"Is it still burning, the lamp on the green mansion?"

The choice of colour was followed by an even greater headache, the choice of a name. I had chosen "Konak-Sultanahmet", but it turned out that a concrete block in the modern part of town had already been registered as the "Konak Hotel" and they opened a lawsuit to force us to change the name. The addition of "Sultanahmet" ought to have sufficed to distinguish the two, but apparently it didn't. We changed it to "Yeşil Konak". To no avail. The term "konak" is a common noun, like chair or table, not a proper name, so no one should be able to claim a monopoly on it. But the Commercial Court upheld their plaint and the bailiffs, quite illegaly, raided the hotel, broke into the depot and carried off all the plates and dishes with the old emblem on them that we had taken out of use and stored there!

We resigned ourselves to our fate and changed the name of the hotel to "Yeşil Ev" (Green House).

After the storm had abated our hotel began to make a highly favourable impression, both the inside and the outside, particularly the outside. Articles and news items began to appear in newspapers and periodicals in several foreign countries.

The response from the world press was due to no publicity or any expense of money or effort on our part (I believe in the old proverb that a good wine needs no bush - especially if it is absolutely unique!).

I must (perhaps rather hesitantly) quote an interesting example of this truth. When Turgut Özal, the President of Turkey in that time, visited the offices of the Washington Post and the New York Times during a visit to the States, not a single line on the subject appeared in the next day's edition of these newspapers. But when representatives of the same newspapers arrived, quite without notice, and took rooms in the Yeşil Ev, they devoted several pages to the hotel, describing it as "shining in Istanbul like a star".

The most interesting of the foreign commentaries is to be found in an article contributed to a travel periodical by the Byzantine scholar and art historian Lord John Julius Norwich:

"Until recently, it has presented a problem in İstanbul: All the places we wanted to see were, on one side, and the big international hotels on the other. And so we were faced with a dilemma; whether to settle into some third-rate fleapit in old Stamboul, knowing that we should at least have the great monuments on our doorstep, or the take refuge on the sanitized heights across the Horn and brave the traffice jams, perhaps half a dozen times a day.

Then, in the early 1980's, something wonderfull happened; Mr. Çelik Gülersoy, director general of the Touring and Automobile Association of Turkey, opened an enchanting little hotel on the edge of the small park that separates the city's most venerable Byzantine church, St. Sophia, from the one of magnificent Islamic monuments, the Sultan Ahmed (Blue) Mosque, The hotel -called the Yeşil Ev, for "Green House"- was an old wooden house of the mid-nineteenth century and in most cities would have been demolished years ago. Saved when already in the last stages of dereliction and decay, it has been lovingly and sensitively restored by Mr. Gülersoy.

To stay there is like staying in the house of an old friend, but with fever social obligations and considerably better room service."

Yeşil Ev had, indeed, introduced the concept of true comfort and hygiene to this "derelict" district and opened a new epoch in Turkish tourism, replacing standardised modernity with historical style. And it was the first time that such a thing had been attempted: An old building in an old district. And with the interior to match.

The favourable opinion voiced by Lord John Julius Norwich has been echoed by all the foreign visitors from 1984 onwards.

With so small capacity, only twenty rooms, it has proved impossible to meet the demand. Some of our customers wait patiently for months.

The crowning event in this favourable response from abroad was the visit paid by the French President Mitterrand at New Year 1992/1993. The reservation was made without revealing the identity of the guest, the rooms being reserved in the name of "a French group". The hotel learned the truth of the matter only half an hour before Mitterrand arrived. There was nothing to be done. Although most of the rooms had been reserved for the President some rooms had also been booked by other travellers.

When the head of the French State arrived, life in Yeşil Ev was going on as usual. Our piano and violin duo was playing light classical music in the narrow lobby (the lobby was later enlarged, at the beginning of 1998, with additional space gained by doing away with two of the rooms on the ground floor). Encountering this scene of domestic music-making the President exclaimed, "In what a lovely place I am!"

Our distinguished guest from the magnificent dining-rooms of the Palais de l'Élysée dined for three days in the Yeşil Ev.

This visit, this incident proved quite conclusively that works produced on a level with Turkey's rich history and true cultural values will meet with true respect and appreciation in the world.

And there was another interesting incident with something of the same significance.

"Europa Nostra" is a famous international association centred in London, and it was by this distinguished association that our Malta Pavilion was awarded the 1980 prize for the high quality of repair and decoration. This was, as far as I know, the first international award ever presented to Turkey. In 1985 it was proposed that the same prize should once again be awarded to the Yeşil Ev, but as it is not the normal custom for the award to be given twice to the same institution, the proposal was withdrawn. In the end, however, the prize was actually awarded, and, strangely enough, through the insistence of the Greek deputy chairman.

This incident provides a very striking example of the basic truth that global peace can only be achieved through regional peace, and through feelings of love and friendship araising from successful and high quality cultural and artistic achievements that combine different peoples by a common bond.

To this globally acknowledged success, we added another, in which we were influential in changing the whole course and fate of Sultanahmet, a district which, by the 1950s, had fallen to the level of a hippy staging-post on the road to Katmandou.

The influence exerted by the Yeşil Ev spread throughout the whole area. The example provided by our hotel, with the music of Mozart playing in the garden, led first of all to the transfer of the prison elsewhere - the first sign of a real change in the local environment.

Then our Association undertook the repair of the old "Medrese" beside the Hotel. It was in a very bad situation, had even snakes resting in its roof!

The historical building was composed juridically from two parts:

The ruined rear side in the State property and totally newly constructed front side in the hands of the individuals!

We began immediately the restoration of the rear side. Observing the approaching danger, the owners of the front side proposed me to sell 5 shops for a very reasonable price to our Association. We rejected this solution with two opinions: To protect the State's interest and to respect the feelings of the first founder of this establishment who had wished to realize here a "Foundation".

But, we have been obliged later, because of the neglect of the attorneys of the Foundations Administration, to pay an amount, ten times more.

The total restoration of the back side has been complated. After finishing the front side's expropriation, the repair of this part has been a real re-construction in its original style. Because this side was exhibiting a chaos of concretes. When the front also gained its original identity, I have recommanded to our Association, to use this historical enviroment as a center of the traditional handicrafts, following the long lasted essential function of "education" of the building. This idea has been accepted and the first example of this kind was born here.

The main aim and a function of this market, in which work is carried on quietly and meticulously throughout the day, is to:

• Revive dying crafts • Give young people the opportunity of acquiring the old skills. • Show visitors and particularily foreign tourists, how these arts and crafts were performed, and • To give the tourist the opportunity of taking with him a true artistic product rather than a number different objets without any quality.

After assuming all the responsibilities and financial costs; the Association also pay annual rent to the State! I think that, all these sacrifices are not very usual in our World.

But these were some of the methods used to steer the environment in a new direction.

We cannot deny that since then a good deal of inferior, cheap kitsch imitations, in no way worthy of the Yeşil Ev, have been produced in the centre behind it. But things will improve with time and, contrary to what holds sway in the economy, "good money will always drive out bad". And the first sign of this was the following:

One day an internationally renowned luxury hotel company arrived in the district to make a global investment in the old empty derelict prison building.

I had been the first person to suggest to Turgut Özal, the Prime Minister of the period, the idea of exploiting the potential offered by the old prison house. At the Official Opening of the Khedive's Summer Palace with his wife when the Head of State, General Evren, carried out the Ceremony, he congratulated me on the restoration and revitalisation work and asked me "what my next project might be?". It was then I mentioned the old prison house, but there was no opportunity to go into it in any detail. On our second meeting, when I was invited to the Officers' Mess at Harbiye to discuss an exhibition arranged by his wife in the US, I had more time to explain the matter. I was again asked the same question and gave the new President the same answer.

Realising that Özal had a rather vague conception of the district I drew a plan. He has not executed my suggestion that the area should be occupied, not by a luxury hotel, but by a cultural centre for the people and that the five acre garden must be used as touristic cafés with pools and music. As a result, this wonderful site was handed over to commercial interests that passed it on from one to the other, but the luxury hotel that finally emerged was, at least in my opinion, better than the old prison-house and constituted an important step in the transformation of the whole destiny of the district.

To realise and exploit with taste and apprecitation the value of a part of the city that houses the palace of the Sultans, the church of St Sophia, the Blue Mosque and the largest covered market in the world; carefully and lovingly to cherish it like a diamond found by chance in a refuse dump and, with all the skill and patience of a jeweller, to polish it and place it in its golden setting - that was my dream, an ideal to which a great contribution was made by the multi-million dollar investment represented by the Four Seasons Hotel.

This contribition is but limited with the fact of the actual situation. Future investment projects, like to arise a new and modern block, in the large garden of the historical building, (following the example and the experience of the Çerağan Palace) and to assume the rantabilty, will badly destroy historical atmosphere of the environment. The erection of a huge building in the neo-classic style in 1840 there was totally wrong. A modern hotel building in the same place will only be a repeate of the same mistake. Today's empty distance between the entrance of the Palace and St. Sophia must be preserved. Aesthetically it needs only a plantation and flowering.

The Yeşil Ev, the first milestone on the road of reform and cultural renaissance, continues to welcome the most select travellers from all parts of the world.

It offers certainly not the comfort on the highest world standard. But it is "civilised" in the best sense of the word, and has the atmosphere of the most select private home.

It gives me really tremendous pleasure to see visitors from all parts of the world enjoy the peace and tranquillity offered by the hotel itself or by the trees and flowers of the paradise garden behind it, an oasis far from the noise and chaos of the city traffic.

And it offers me one of the greatest "consolations" of my pretty well suffering life.

While they are eating or drinking coffee in this peaceful and tranquil environment to the immortal strains of classical music, I gaze, with moistened eyes, at the pool in the centre and see a romantic little boy sitting on the pink porphyry basin on a hot summer afternoon reading his first novels, my picture from sixty years ago.

After so many years, and after so many sweet and bitter experiences, and after actually living so many novels, I stop to meditate on a fate and destiny that made it possible for me to bring a monumental pool from a palace in Yıldız to an old neglected garden belonging to a mansion of the same nobility of character, in Sultanahmet, and I believe that all these conceals of a mysterious significance cannot be explained by chance or mere personal ability.

ILLUSTRATIONS

THE WORLD OF THE "KONAK"S IN YESTERDAY'S İSTANBUL

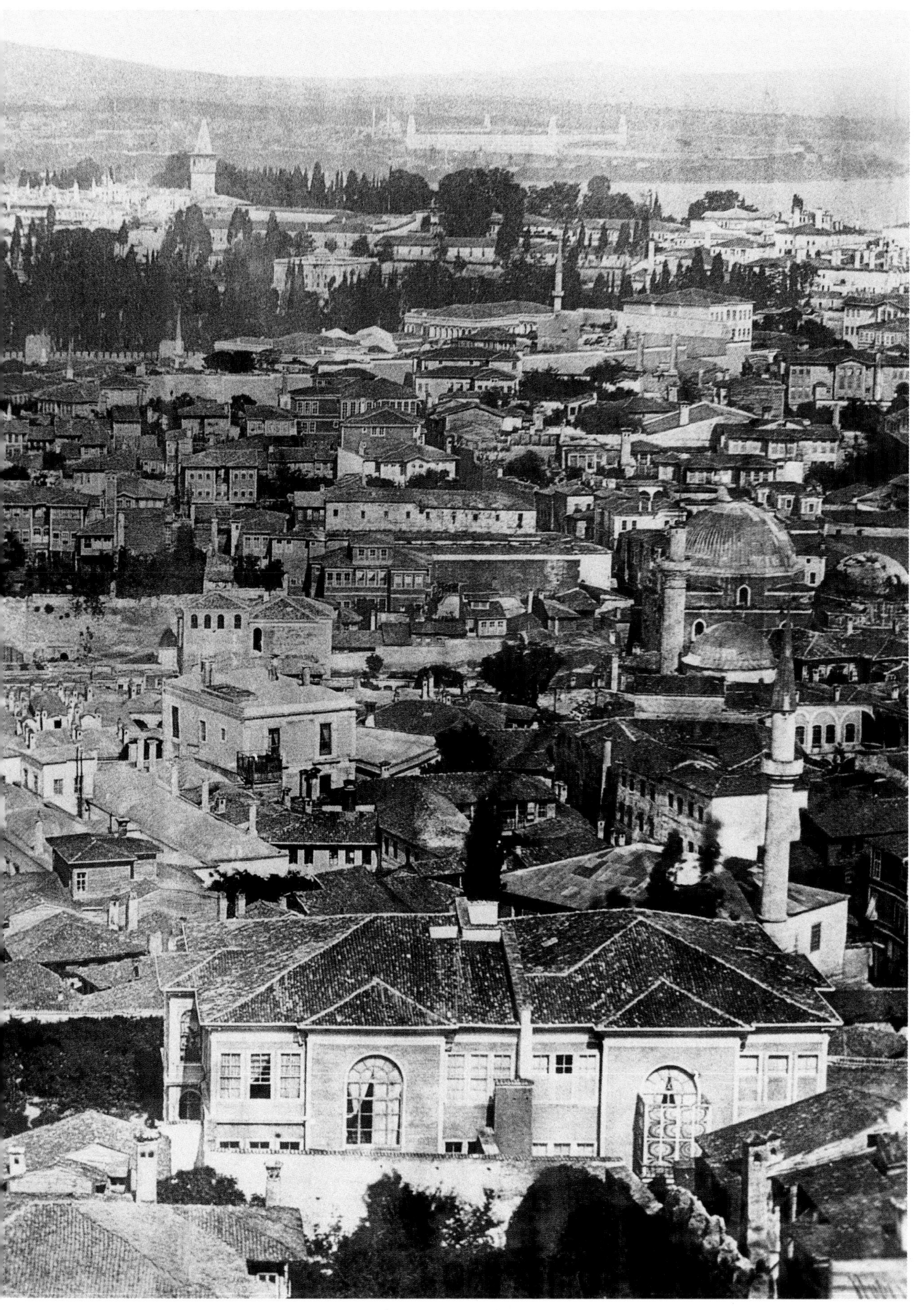

One of the rare and first photographs of old İstanbul, 1850's. Taken by Robertson. From Beyazıt Tower to the Palace.

The all green and characteristic İstanbul. Cerrahpaşa district. On the left Marmara Sea. Beginning of the century.

Destruction of the fire. 1921/22.

Not far from Yeşil Ev:
Two original konaks on the Alemdar Street, leading from Gülhane Park to Sultanahmet Square. On the left, the Soğukkuyu Medresesi. still existing. The Konak in the center is not existing anymore. Some concrete buildings are unfortunately constructed on its place. The Konak on the right is rebuilt last year, but unfortunately in a different style.
A rare picture from the Constitutional Period (1910's), showing Sultan Reşad on his way to Ayasofya for Friday Prayer.

My first meetings with Sultanahmet area. 1951.

The Konak in 1960's.

THE FALL OF THE KONAK

1970'S

The west side in 1977.

The entrance hall and the passage to the garden.

"No comment". 1982.

The rooms of the first floor.

The garden during the reconstruction of the house.

The east side of the front. (Today's shop).

THE RESSURECTION

1984

A very new house: Yeşil Ev. And his "next-door": The unbelievable Blue Mosque!

Interior

The entrance hall and the passage to the garden.

The Art - Nouveau lamp (from the Palace of the "Serasker").

THE RESTAURANTS

The part of the first restaurant looking on the street side.

The old restaurant.

"A room with a view"

A corner in the old part of the restaurant.

New opened part of the restaurant.

New opened (1998) part of the restaurant.

The rooms

One of the rooms at the 1. floor.

One of the rooms at the 2. floor.

The "Pasha's Room"

Pasha's room and its bath.

THE GARDEN

The garden in the autumn.

In springtime.

"Selsebil"

The byzantine cistern.

Souvenirs from the older times:
Above: The last part of the "Serasker"s Palace in Yıldız, where the pool was originally located.
Belowe: The child Ç.G. who was reading his first books at the steps of the pool. 1930's.

THE SERA - RESTAURANT

The medrese

(HANDICRAFTS CENTER)

"No comment" again. The Medrese in 1983.

The new construction of the Konak and the dilapileted Medresse, next to it.
On the right original structure of Medresse. On the left side the illegally sold front of it to the individuals. 1983.

Terribly changed front of the Medresse by new constructions.

Partly restoration of Medrese. The front part on the right is waiting for the expropriation formalities. 1985 situation.

Resurrection of the Medrese.1986

In its new life: A center of the old İstanbul handicrafts.

The front of the building (Reconstructed).

In the autumn...

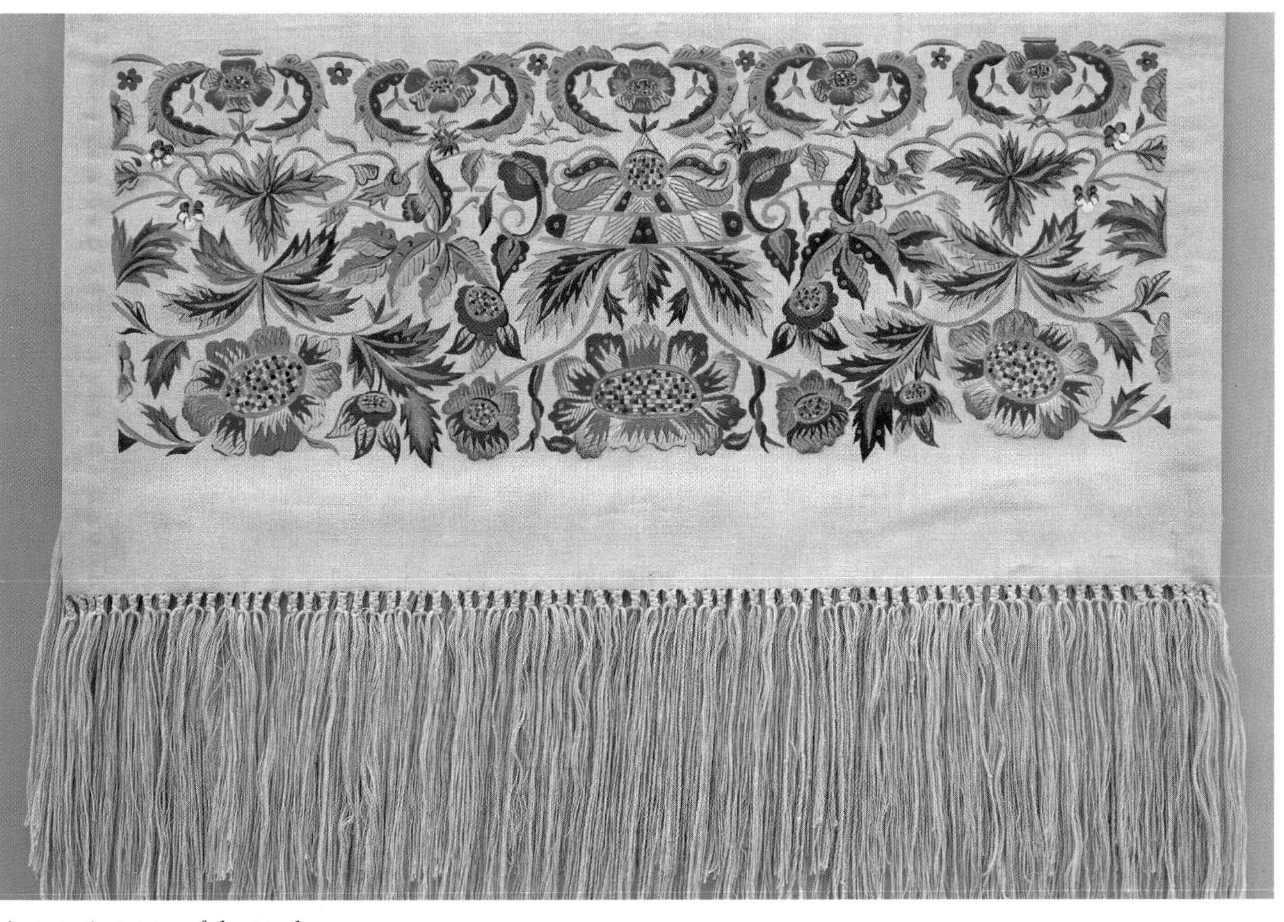

Artistic Activities of the Market.

The author of Yeşil Ev.

ACKNOWLEDGEMENTS

The Architect Mustafa Pehlivanoğlu (Techn. Univ. İst.) (İTÜ)

The Construction Mustafa and Vasıf Pehlivanoğlu

The Director Veli Yavuz

The Musicians of the Hotel
Violin: İsmail Temel
Piano: Hüseyin Coşkun

Reception
Gazanfer Kızıldemir
Onur Tuntaş
Aydın Tümen

Service
İlhan Çelenk
Aydın Akbaş
Ayhan Çakır
Yaşar Arslan
Cemal Bekmezci
Mustafa Uzun
Cahit Kepil
Hüseyin Akdemir

The Cuisine
Hayrettin Ünyılmaz
Zekeriya Çelen
Ali Şahbaz
İsa Tan
Ömer Şirin
Ali Öğütçü

Comptability
Yılmaz Ayaz
Tamer Topal
Celal Tur

Floors
Kâtip Uzunkaya
Remziye Bunyak
Hüsnü Gündoğan
Ensar Aksu
Âlim Demir

Technicians
Hüseyin Temel
Haydar Şahbaz

Driver Eren Tüzel

The door Cemil Özmen

EUROPA
NOSTRA

ISTANBUL — HOTEL KONAK

FOR THE RECONSTRUCTION OF AN
IMPORTANT 19TH CENTURY MANSION,
NOW A BEAUTIFUL EXAMPLE OF
CONSERVATION IN THIS CITY

PHOTOGRAPHS

	Pages
Çelik Gülersoy	: Cover and 3, 39, 51, 53, 57, 58, 70 (below)
From Ç.G.'s Archive	: 17, 18-19, 20-21, 22, 23, 25-29, 59, 67
Mustafa Dorsay	: 31, 35, 36-37, 38 (above), 40-41, 44, 45, 46-47,48, 54-55,
Mustafa Erem Çalıkoğlu	: 33, 34, 42, 43, 60, 61, 62
Kayhan Çağlayan Yılmaz Dinç	: 68-69, 70 (above), 71
Ömer Kırkpınar	: 72 (Portrait of Ç.G.)